The things we use

Sally Hewitt and Jane Rowe

Evans

About this book

The LOOK AROUND YOU books have been put together in a way that makes them ideal for teachers and parents to share with young children. Take time over each question and project. Have fun learning about how all sorts of different homes, clothes, toys and everyday objects have been designed for a special purpose.

THE THINGS WE USE deals with the kinds of ideas about design and technology that many children will be introduced to in their early years at school. The pictures and text will encourage children to explore design on the page, and all around them. This book will help them to understand some of the basic rules about why objects are a certain shape, why they are made from particular materials, and why they work well and are easy to use. It will also help them to develop their own design skills.

The 'eye opener' boxes reveal interesting and unusual facts, or lead children to examine one aspect of design. There are also activities that put theory into practice in an entertaining and informative way. Children learn most effectively by joining in, talking, asking questions and solving problems, so encourage them to talk about what they are doing and to find ways of solving the problems for themselves.

Try to make thinking about design and technology a part of everyday life. Just pick up any object around the house and talk about why it has been made that way, and how it could be improved. Design is not just a subject for adults. You can have a lot of fun with it at any age - and develop artistic flair and practical skills.

Contents

The things we use

What do you **do** every day?
You are probably **busy** from morning until night.

Here are some **things** you might use each day.

Can you think of other things that you **use?**

All of these things have to be **safe** to use and do their job well.

For example, a good mug must have a **strong** handle and not **break** easily.

The mugs below are quite **unusual**.

Can you see why they would be **difficult** to use?

This book will tell you about some of the things we use **every day**.

7

Carrying

What would happen if you tried to **carry** all these things to school without a bag?

This **rucksack** is good for carrying lots of things and leaves your hands free.

What kind of **bag** do you carry your things to school in?

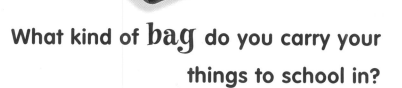

Design a folder

Make your own folder from card to carry your notes or drawings to school in.

1. Measure the largest piece of paper you want to put in the folder, so you know how big your folder must be.

2. In pencil, draw a plan on your card as shown. Cut out the shape.

3. Fold along the dotted lines. Keep the lines on the outside of the folder, so that you can see them. Rub out the lines when you have finished folding.

4. Glue the pieces together at the sides.

5. Decorate the folder in any way you like!

19

Telephones

A telephone is used by **four** parts of the body – your ear, your mouth, your hand and your finger!

Why would these strange-looking **telephones** be difficult to use?

The numbers on a telephone are always set out like this. The number 5 sometimes has one or two raised bumps near it to help blind people to dial.

➡ You need both **hands** to use this old-fashioned phone.

⬆ This phone has a **screen** so you can see the person you are talking to.

⬆ You can carry this **mobile** phone around in your pocket.

⬅ What **animal** do you think this telephone is supposed to be?

On wheels

You can see **wheels** all around you.
They are used for lots of **different** things.

➡ The wheels on this baby buggy **swivel**
round so that it can move in different
directions.

◀ You can **pull** this suitcase along on
wheels when it is full of heavy clothes.

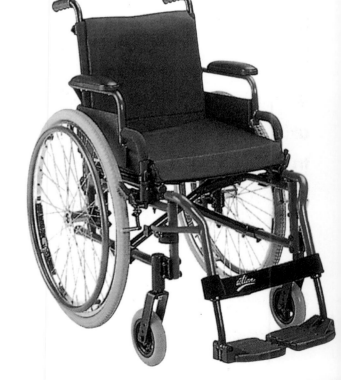

➡ The wheels on this wheelchair are
turned around using your **hands.**

Make a truck with wheels that go round

Wheels turn around on a rod, which is called an axle.

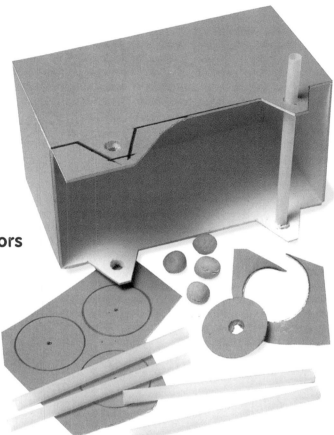

You will need:
* ✳ A small box ✳ 1 or 2 drinking straws
* ✳ Card ✳ Plasticine or Blu-tack ✳ Scissors

1. Cut a truck shape out of your box as shown.

2. Get an adult to help you push a hole through each triangle shape with scissors.

3. Cut four wheels out of your card. Make a hole in the middle of each one.

4. Cut your straws to make two axles that are wider than your truck. Push them through the holes in the triangles and put a wheel and a blob of plasticine on each end.

5. Think of ways to decorate your truck.

Bedtime

The **beds** on these pages are made for different people.

Cots stop **babies** from rolling out when they are asleep.

A **camp bed** can be packed away so that it can be carried easily.

How many types of **material** can you see in this bedroom?

What materials are your pillow, mattress and bedcovers **made** of? What do they **feel** like?

You probably use a soft pillow.

In some places people prefer stone headrests, like this one from long ago.

Amazing designs

All of these objects do an everyday job, but look how **imaginatively** they have been designed!

This unusual chair has been shaped out of **metal**. How comfortable do you think it would be?

This crocodile is made to hold **toast** in his back and **butter** in his mouth!

How easy do you think this *juicer* would be to use? How would you **catch** all the juice?

Look at the twig below. Did you **guess** that it is really a coloured pencil? Look around and try to find more **amazing designs** in the things you use every day.

Index